Crocheted Sun Hat
&
Bucket Hat

by

Janis Frank

Page 2

Thank you for purchasing this book. This book remains the copyrighted property of the author, and may not be redistributed to others for commercial or non-commercial purposes. If you enjoyed this book, please encourage your friends to purchase their own copy from their favourite book retailer.

Thank you for your support and respecting the hard work of this author. The purchase of this book allows you to make and sell the physical items you create.

Copyright 2023 by Janis Frank

All rights reserved.

Page 6

Table of Contents

Things You Need .... Page 11

Gauge .... Page 12

Make the:

    Small/Medium Hat .... Page 12

    Large/Extra Large Hat .... Page 16

    Band .... Page 19

    Flower .... Page 21

    Leaf .... Page 24

Hints and Tips .... Page 26

Abbreviations .... Page 30

Help Support My Work .... Page 31

More FREE Crochet Patterns .... Page 31

Follow Me on Social Media .... Page 33

Gussy it up or wear it plain, this crocheted hat pattern is extremely versatile and makes hats for nearly anyone. Anyone but my 14 year old son apparently, who said, with his usual unenthusiastic honesty, "I don't like it but it fits OK". How do I know this? I needed to borrow his head to see how the smaller size fit and felt when wearing, so I guess it's at least fit approved ¯_('~')_/¯

This hat can be made a number of ways, either as a wider brimmed sun hat with a flower, plain with the brim shaped similar to a cowboy/cowgirl hat, or with a narrower brim to be a bucket hat. Any way you choose is going to be a success! It's easy to make, and as long as you know the basics of crochet. Literally if you know how to chain, single crochet (sc) and do a slip stitch (sl st), you'll be able to make the hat. The flower can be a bit more tricky but I've included photos and detailed descriptions to help you along.

The hat is made with 2 strands worsted weight yarn (or one strand of super bulky yarn) and a larger crochet hook. The stitches need to be fairly tight so the hat will hold it's shape. Anything larger than the gauge given will make it floppy and the sizing may not work out as written. But, like all my patterns, play with it! If you want a floppy hat, no one said you can't.

There aren't any specific measurements for the hat sizing. It's all very general as there is some stretch to the hat when finished and will form to fit the head it's covering. If you want your hat to fit a little looser, go for the bigger size.

The way I thought of it when I was designing this hat, if it fit the glass head, it's a small/medium size. In other words, a regular sized head. If it fits me and looks a little too big on the glass head, it's a large/extra large. Let me put it this way. I know I have a big head. If you have ever thought you too might have a big head because hats don't always fit you, hello fellow large head! If this statement makes no sense to you, go for the small/medium.

Things You Need

6 mm (US 10 or J) crochet hook (or what ever size hook you need to get the correct gauge)

3.5 mm (US 4 or E) crochet hook for top edging, flowers and leaves (all optional)

2 balls Worsted Weight yarn or 1 ball Super Bulky yarn (for the hat itself)

>For the sun hat you'l need:
>
>106 gr or 3.7 oz *each* of the worsted weight colours (216 m or 237 yards)
>
>> *or*
>
>173 gr or 6 oz Super Bulky yarn (170 m or 185 yards)
>
>of course it's less yarn for the bucket hat.

Worsted weight yarn (for band, flowers, leaves and edging)

Stitch markers (at least 8 but it never hurts to have more. See Hints and Tips section)

Tapestry needle (to sew band and flowers, work in the ends)

Gauge

With 2 strands of worsted weight yarn *or* 1 strand of super bulky yarn

13 sts = 4"

14 rows = 4"

Check your gauge to obtain correct sizing and density of the final fabric created. The stitching needs to be tight to hold the hat shape.

Small/Medium

With 2 strands of worsted weight yarn *or* 1 strand of super bulky yarn **and** your 6 mm (US 10 or J) crochet hook...

Ch 2 (make the first chain large enough to fit in all the stitches for Round 1)

Round 1: 12sc around. Do NOT join. The following rounds are worked without joining.

Round 2: Sc in first sc of previous round. 2sc in the next stitch. *Sc in next stitch. 2sc in the next stitch.* Repeat from * to * around. Place stitch marker. (18 sts)

Round 3: *2sc. 2sc in the next stitch.* Repeat from * to * around to stitch marker.

Round 4: *3sc. 2sc in the next stitch.* Repeat from * to * around to stitch marker.

Round 5: *4sc. 2sc in the next stitch.* Repeat from * to * around to stitch marker.

Round 6: *5sc. 2sc in the next stitch.* Repeat from * to * around to stitch marker.

Round 7: *3sc. 2sc in the next stitch. 2sc. 2sc in the next stitch.* Repeat from * to * around to stitch marker. (54 sts)

Round 8: *4sc. 2sc in the next stitch. 3sc. 2sc in the next stitch.* Repeat from * to * around to stitch marker. (66 sts)

Round 9: Sc around in the back loop.

*Crochet in the **BACK LOOP***

Round 10-20: Sc around.

Page 14

Round 21: *5sc. 2sc in the next stitch.* Repeat from * to * around to stitch marker. (77 sts)

***Please note** - If you are making the *BUCKET HAT,* crochet these stitches as you normally would (through both loops of the stitch).

- If you are making the *SUN HAT*, crochet these stitches through the front loop ONLY)

Round 22: *8sc. 2sc in the next stitch. 9sc. 2sc in the next stitch.* Repeat from * to * around. Sc in the last st. (or crochet as many stitches as you have at the end of the round). (Mark each increase with a stitch marker as you go for a total of 8 markers. You will use these later on. I'm no longer giving final stitch counts. See the [Hints and Tips](#) section for clarification if needed).

Round 23: 4sc. 2sc in the next stitch. *9sc. 2sc in the next stitch.* Repeat from * to * around (Crochet as many stitches as you have to the end of the round but there should be 0).

Round 24: *10sc. 2sc in the next stitch. 11sc. 2sc in the next stitch.* Repeat from * to * around. 2sc (or crochet as many stitches as you have to the end of the round).

***Please note** – If you are making the *BUCKET HAT* sc around and continue on the Round 31.

Round 25: 5sc. 2sc in the next stitch. *11sc. 2sc in the next stitch. 12sc. 2sc in the next stitch.* Repeat from * to * around 2 *more* times. 11sc. 2sc in the next stitch. 8sc. (or crochet as many stitches as you have to the end of the round).

Round 26: Sc around.

Round 27: *Sc to the next stitch marker. Sc as you normally would. Sc to the next stitch marker. 2sc in this stitch.* Repeat from * to * around.

Other ways to state this round...Increase 4 times evenly around. Or...Increase every other stitch marker.

Round 28: Sc around.

Round 29: *Sc to the next stitch marker. 2sc in this stitch. Sc to the next stitch marker. Sc as you normally would.* Repeat from * to * around.

Round 30: Sc around and join with a slip stitch. Tie off and break yarn.

Round 31: With the inside of the hat facing you and with *one strand of worsted weight yarn* and the same hook you made the hat with, sc around. Join with a slip st. Tie off and break yarn.

Top or Crown Edging (Optional)

With 3.5 mm (US 4 or E) crochet hook and a *single strand of worsted weight yarn*...
In the loops left from Round 9, sc in each stitch around. Join with a slip st. Tie off and break yarn.

Work in all ends.

Large/Extra Large

With 2 strands of worsted weight yarn *or* 1 strand of super bulky yarn ***and*** your 6 mm (US 10 or J) crochet hook...

Ch 2 (make the first chain large enough to fit in all the stitches for Round 1)

Round 1: 12sc around. Do NOT join. The following rounds are worked without joining.
Round 2: Sc in first sc of previous round. 2sc in the next stitch. *Sc in next stitch. 2sc in the next stitch.* Repeat from * to * around. Place stitch marker. (18 sts)
Round 3: *2sc. 2sc in the next stitch.* Repeat from * to * around to stitch marker.
Round 4: *3sc. 2sc in the next stitch.* Repeat from * to * around to stitch marker.
Round 5: *4sc. 2sc in the next stitch.* Repeat from * to * around to stitch marker.
Round 6: *5sc. 2sc in the next stitch.* Repeat from * to * around to stitch marker.
Round 7: *3sc. 2sc in the next stitch. 2sc. 2sc in the next stitch.* Repeat from * to * around to stitch marker. (54 sts)
Round 8: *5sc. 2sc in the next stitch.* Repeat from * to * around to stitch marker. (63 sts)
Round 9: *8sc. 2sc in the next stitch.* Repeat from * to * around to stitch marker. (70 sts)
Round 10: Sc around in the back loop.

*Crochet in the **BACK LOOP***

Round 11-23: Sc around.

Round 24: *4sc. 2sc in the next stitch.* Repeat from * to * around to stitch marker. (84 sts)

Please note - If you are making the ***BUCKET HAT, crochet these stitches as you normally would (through both loops of the stitch).

- If you are making the ***SUN HAT***, crochet these stitches through the front loop ONLY)

Round 25: *9sc. 2sc in the next stitch. 10sc. 2sc in the next stitch.* Repeat from * to * around to the beginning of the row. (Mark each increase with a stitch marker as you go for a total of 8 markers. You will use these later on. I'm no longer giving final stitch counts. See the Hints and Tips section for clarification if needed).

Round 26: 6sc. 2sc in the next stitch. *11sc. 2sc in the next stitch. 10sc. 2sc in the next stitch.* Repeat from * to * around 2 *more* times. 10sc. 2sc in the next stitch. 5sc. (or crochet as many stitches as you have to the end of the round).

Round 27: *11sc. 2sc in the next stitch. 12sc. 2sc in the next stitch.* Repeat from * to * around 3 *more* times.

***Please note** – If you are making the **BUCKET HAT** sc around and continue on the Round 34.

Round 28: 6sc. 2sc in the next stitch. *12sc. 2sc in the next stitch. 13sc. 2sc in the next stitch.* Repeat from * to * around 2 *more* times. 12sc. 2sc in the next stitch. 7sc. (or crochet as many stitches as you have to the end of the round).
Round 29: Sc around.
Round 30: *Sc to the next stitch marker. Sc as you normally would. Sc to the next stitch marker. 2sc in this stitch.* Repeat from * to * around.

Other ways to state this round...Increase 4 times evenly around. Or...Increase every other stitch marker.

Round 31: Sc around.
Round 32: *Sc to the next stitch marker. 2sc in this stitch. *Sc to the next stitch marker. Sc as you normally would.* Repeat from * to * around.
Round 33: Sc around and join with a slip stitch. Tie off and break yarn.
Round 34: With the inside of the hat facing you and with *one strand of worsted weight yarn* and the same hook you made the hat with, sc around. Join with a sl st. Tie off and break yarn.

Top or Crown Edging (Optional)

With 3.5 mm (US 4 or E) crochet hook and *a single strand of worsted weight yarn...*
In the loops left from Round 10, sc in each stitch around. Join with a slip st. Tie off and break yarn.

Work in all ends.

*Take a photo of this QR code
for more FREE crochet patterns!*

Band (Optional)

With a *single strand of worsted weight yarn* and your large 6mm (US 10 or J) crochet hook:
Small/Medium - Chain 74
Large/Extra Large - Chain 79

In second chain from hook, sc in each chain. Bring the ends of the band together and sc in the first sc of previous row. Be sure not to twist. We are now working in rounds.
Round 2-3: Sc around. Join with a slip st. Tie off and break yarn.

Working in the bottom loop of the original chains...

Work 3 rounds of sc evenly. Join with a slip st. Tie off and break yarn. Work in ends. Attach to the hat sewing the bottom edge of the band to where the brim joins the hat.

Add flowers or other embellishments of your choice.

Flower (Optional)

Using 3 or 4 colours of worsted weigh yarn

3.5 mm (US E or 4) crochet hook

Ch 2 (make the first chain large enough to fit in all the stitches for Round 1)

Round 1: With the centre colour of your choice, 10sc in 2nd chain from hook. Join with sl st in first sc. Break yarn. Tie off.

Round 2: With the 2nd colour of your choice (middle of the petals), join in any sc. 2sc in same st as join, 2sc around. Join with sl st to 1st sc of the round.

Round 3: Ch 1. Sc in same st as join. *Ch 4. Starting in 2nd ch from hook, sc in each chain. (3sc total). Join with sl st in the starting sc of the Ch 4. Sc in the next 2 stitches. Ch 5. Starting in 2nd ch from hook, sc in each chain. (4sc total). Join with sl st in the starting sc of the Ch 5. Sc in the next 2 stitches.* Repeat from * to * around, ending with 1sc instead of the 2sc. Join with sl st to 1st sc of the round. Break yarn. Tie off.

Round 3 completed

Round 4: Working in the ***Ch 4 petals only***! And with your third colour choice... Join with sl st in 1st sc before Ch 4 petal. *In the bottom loops of the chain from the previous round, sc, hdc in 1st loop. Hdc, dc in the 2nd loop, 2dc in the 3rd loop. In the top loop, 2dc, ch 2 sl st in 2nd chain from hook, 2dc. Working on the other edge of the petal, 2dc in the 1st st, dc, hdc in the 2nd st, hdc, sc in the 3rd st. Sl st in the sl st of the previous round. Hold the next Ch 5 petal back, sc in the next 2nd sc between the Ch 5 and the next Ch 4 petal.* Repeat from * to * around. Join with sl st in the 1st sc of the round. Break yarn. Tie off.

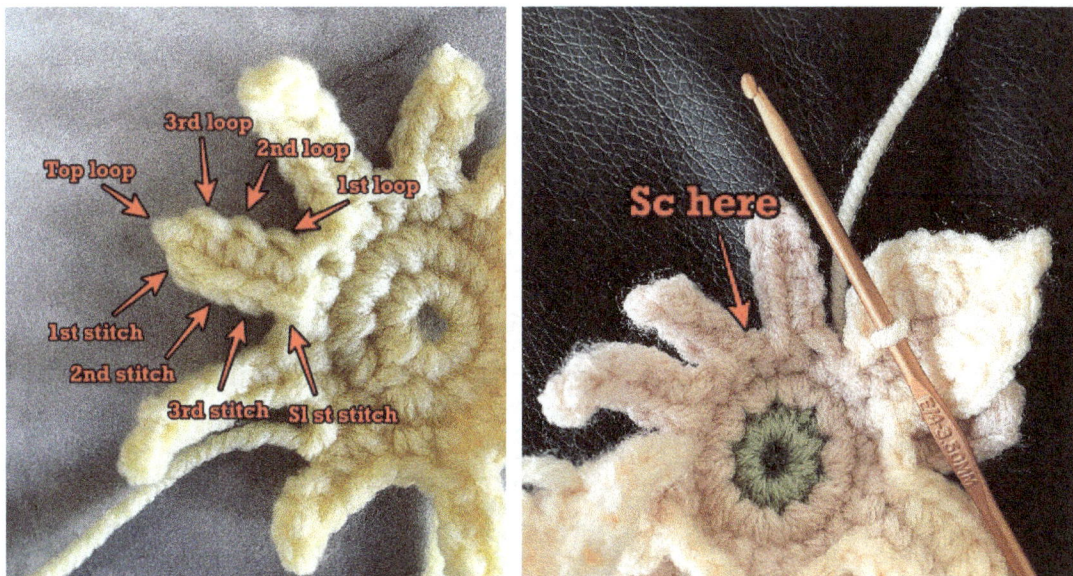

Round 5: Working in the *Ch 5 petals only*! And with your third (or fourth) colour choice...

Join with a sl st to the 1st loop of the chain. *2sc in the same loop, 2hdc in the 2nd loop, 2dc in the 3rd and 4th loops. In the top loop, 2dc, ch 2 sl st in 2nd chain from hook, 2dc. Working on the other edge of the petal, 2dc in the 1st and 2nd sts, 2hdc in the 3rd st, 2sc in the 4th st. Ch1. Hold the ch 4 petal forward and working in the next ch 5 petal.* Repeat from * to * around. Join with a sl st to the 1st sc of the round. Break yarn. Tie off. Work in all the ends. Attach to the hat.

Leaf (Optional)

Using worsted weigh yarn (small quantities from your stash)

3.5 mm (US E or 4) crochet hook.

Stitch marker. (A piece of yarn or bobby pin will do).

Please note: The rounds end in various places on the bottom of the leaf. Regardless, the stitch counts work. Round 4 evens out the stitches giving the leaf shape.

Ch 2 (make the first chain large enough to fit in all the stitches for Round 1)

Round 1: 11sc in 2nd chain from hook. Do *NOT* join. Begin to work in the round.

Round 2: In the 1st sc from the last round, sc. 2sc in the next st. In the next st, sc, hdc. In the next st, hdc, dc. 2dc in the next 2 sts. In the next st, dc, hdc. In the next st, hdc, sc. 2sc in the next st. Sc.

Round 3: *2sc in the next st, sc* Repeat from * to * 2 *more* times. In the next st, sc, hdc. (Mark the hdc with a stitch marker). In the next st, hdc, dc. 2dc in the next st. In the next st, dc, trc. In the next st, trc, dc. 2dc in the next st. In the next st, dc, hdc. In the next st, hdc, sc. *Sc, 2sc in the next st* Repeat from * to * 2 *more* times.

Round 4: *2sc, 2sc in the next st* Repeat from * to * 2 *more* times. (Or as many sc as you need to get to the stitch marker). Sc in the stitch marked with the marker. As you normally would, proceed as follows, hdc, 4dc. In the next st (the 1st trc from the previous round), dc, trc. Ch 2 sl st in the 2nd chain from hook. In the next st, trc, dc. As you normally would, proceed as follows, 4dc, hdc, sc. *2sc, 2sc in the next st* Repeat from * to * 4 *more* times. 2Sc. Sl st in the next st. Break yarn. Tie off.

Work in the ends and sew into place.

Hints and Tips

Colour choice of the 2 different worsted weight yarns can make a huge difference to your final hat. I mixed 2 tones of one colour for the cowboy/cowgirl hat, white and beige for the yellow flower hat, camo and black for the camo bucket hat. Variegated yarns should be used with a solid colour of yarn for the best effect.

Stitch markers make this so much easier. Pieces of yarn also work. I like to use a single bobby pin to note where the round starts and use regular stitch markers for where I'm making the increases.

In regards to the stitch markers, if you don't want to use the stitch counts given for the rows, you can use the stitch markers instead. Think of it as *increase 8 times evenly around.* I did the math to figure out what was even spacing and to stagger the increases between the rows around the brim for the crochet purists.

I like to move my *start of the round* stitch marker as I make each row (the bobby pin in the photos). I leave the increases for the brim where they are. It makes things go a little quicker and avoids keeping track of stitch counts.

Speaking of stitch counts. This is crocheted in the round, meaning if your stitch counts become a little off, too many or not enough between the increases, it will still work out in the long run. I gave the number of stitches between the increases mainly to avoid repeating increases along the brim. It looked very noticeable and unsightly to me when the increases in increases lined up, but I'm a bit of a stickler for things like that. If you could care less how it look, have at it!

Edging is done with worsted weight yarn! If you are using a double strand of worsted weight yarn, select one of the colours and go with that. If you are using Super Bulky yarn, you'll need to use any complimentary colour of worsted weight yarn you like. You don't need very much.

Why I made the band the way I did. It's very easy to twist the band if you join the chain right away. It's considerably easier to avoid this if you sc in each chain first then bring the ends together.

Advice for working in the ends of the flowers. It's easier to hold the yarn to the back of your work and catch the yarn for 4 or 5 sts as you are making the flower. It works the ends in automatically and involves less to work in at the end.

As much as I wanted to avoid pressing anything, the leaves and flowers need to be pressed to lie flat. Be sure to do a test swatch **BEFORE** you press anything. Acrylic is notorious for melting and losing all constructive properties when pressed. It melts to give a flat, melted look. Press with your iron at the lowest setting possible. Press with a *damp cloth* between the iron and the flower petals or leaf. Iron the flower petals and leaves from the ***BACK***.

It's not overly important where you single crochet between the petals on Round 4. As long as it's only 1sc and consistent.

I like to stagger where I join the next colour of yarn to make the flower. That way the joins and end points don't all congest at one point.

Use as many flowers and leaves on the hat as you like! I was going to make a hat entirely surrounded by flowers and leaves but I had to draw a line somewhere with the examples. I already made 7 hats and I had to cut myself off. I'm pretty sure I'm going to make one regardless, and put it in my Etsy shop :-)

Add extra embroidered details to the flowers, hat, leaves and band as you see fit. I made the blue/yellow flower with one solid colour in the middle and inside leaves to see what it would look like. I didn't like it so did some quick stitches around to make it green.

The cowboy/cowgirl hat is the sun hat but with the brim formed into a more familiar cowboy hat style.

The band on the cowboy/cowgirl hat has daisy chain embellishments. You can either embroider them on or use your crochet hook. Place your yarn at the back of the band and pull up a loop to the front. Push your hook through the next hole and pull up a loop. Keep going down the length of the band.

Though the flower is made with yarn in this example, I originally designed it to be made with crochet cotton thread and a small crochet hook. You can add it to a band and make a bracelet with it. I have a number of bracelet designs that it will work with Waves Bracelet, Fans Bracelet Pattern, Quick Crochet Bracelet and my Friendship Flower Bracelet. The last one has a flower already made for it but you could easily switch that flower out for this one.

I'm not making any promises, but I do hope to post other flowers and leaves on my website. I have a number of different designs I'd like to get on there. At the moment I have two flowers (3 if you count the one included with my crocheted slippers) that you can take a look at. The flowers are done with crochet cotton thread and I'm not sure how large the final flower would be when made with yarn. I'll leave that up to you. The one that would also work with the yarn is my Free Crochet Flower Pattern. It should be slightly smaller than the flower I designed to go with the hat.

Here are the QR codes to all the bracelets, flowers and slippers to scan if you'd like to see them. Take a photo with your phone or tablet and the link will pop right up to take you there.

Quick Bracelet

Fans Bracelet

Crochet Slippers

Crochet Flower

Flower Bracelet

Waves Bracelet

Abbreviations

Ch - chain

sc – single crochet

sl st – slip stitch

hdc – half double crochet

dc – double crochet

trc – treble crochet

st – stitch

sts – stitches

Like all of my patterns you have my permission to sell and/or give away the physical items that you make using this pattern. You are NOT permitted to reprint this pattern in any form unless you have obtained my written permission to do so.

If you have any questions, please feel free to leave a comment or send me your questions at kweenbee_crafts@hotmail.ca.

Help Support My Work!

Follow me on TikTok, Instagram, Twitter, Facebook, Pinterest and YouTube. Every follow, subscribe, thumbs up, like, heart and share help increase my popularity on the web and get more viewers to my work. It costs you nothing but helps me sooooo much!

If you would like to help a little more, you can always support me on Patreon or you can make a single time donation at Buy Me a Coffee.

If you love this pattern, be sure to check out my website KweenBee.com.

More FREE crochet patterns on my website

This is the latest list of patterns I have on my website. It is an ever growing list so you might want to click the following link to check out my Free Crochet Patterns page and **KweenBee.com.** I design new patterns as I get time and add them to my website.

To make it even easier, you can take a photo of the QR code below with your phone or tablet. It will take you right to the webpage!

Take a photo of this QR code
for more FREE crochet patterns!

If you would like to access any of the patterns you can easily do an internet search to find them. When you are on your favourite search engine like Google, Bing, Yahoo, etc. Enter the term ***Kweenbee*** and the title as it is written below (capitalization isn't important). It will pop up for you in the search results and be super-easy to find.

For example, enter it like this:

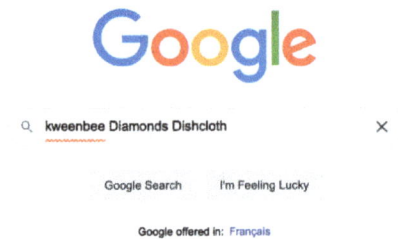

Your results will have my pattern at the very top...usually. Depending on the popularity of the pattern, you may get a link to Pinterest or Ravelry first. Don't worry! All of those options have links back to my original patterns, too!

Quick Crochet Bracelet

How to Crochet Jewelry – Make a Friendship Flower Bracelet

How to Crochet Slippers for Children and Adults

How to Crochet Jewelry – Waves Bracelet

Crochet a Skull and Crossbones Dishcloth

How to Crochet – Free Crochet Flower Pattern

How to Crochet – Fans Bracelet Pattern

How to Crochet an Afghan…or How to Do Tunisian Crochet

How to Crochet Jewelry – Make a Victorian Steampunk Necklace and Bracelet

How to Crochet a Dishcloth – A Beginner's Pattern

Follow Me on Social Media

[Me on Pinterest](http://www.pinterest.com/kweenbee_crafts) - http://www.pinterest.com/kweenbee_crafts

[Like Me on Facebook](https://www.facebook.com/janis.the.knitter/) - https://www.facebook.com/janis.the.knitter/

[Me on YouTube](https://www.youtube.com/user/KweenBeeCrafts) - https://www.youtube.com/user/KweenBeeCrafts

[Instagram](https://www.instagram.com/janis_as_in_joplin) - https://www.instagram.com/janis_as_in_joplin

[Twitter](https://twitter.com/Crafty_Janis) - https://twitter.com/Crafty_Janis

KweenBee.com

[My Etsy Shop](http://www.etsy.com/shop/KweenBee) - http://www.etsy.com/shop/KweenBee

[Become a Patron on Patreon!](https://www.patreon.com/JanisFrank) - https://www.patreon.com/JanisFrank

[Buy Me a Coffee](https://www.buymeacoffee.com/JanisFrank) - https://www.buymeacoffee.com/JanisFrank

Copyright 2023
All rights reserved
Janis Frank

Notes

www.ingramcontent.com/pod-product-compliance
Lightning Source LLC
Chambersburg PA
CBHW081130080526
44587CB00021B/3815